MW01265180

Animal Skeletons

BY JUDITH JANDA PRESNALL

ANIMAL SKELETONS

ILLUSTRATED BY KRISTIN KEST

FRANKLIN WATTS
A Division of Grolier Publishing
New York/London/Hong Kong/Sydney
Danbury, Connecticut

To My Son, Kory

Library of Congress Cataloging-in-Publication Data

Presnall, Judith Janda.
    Animal skeletons / by Judith Janda Presnall illustrated by
Kristin Kest.
        p.   cm.
    Includes bibliographical references and index.
    Summary: Compares the skeletons of different kinds of animals,
describing their various forms and functions and providing related
activities for each chapter.
    ISBN 0-531-11160-1
    1. Skeleton—Juvenile literature.   [1. Skeleton.   2. Bones.
3. Anatomy, Comparative.]   I. Kest, Kristin, ill.   II. Title.
QL821.P74   1995
591.4'71—dc20   95-35269
                                                                CIP
                                                                 AC

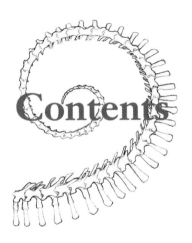

Contents

one
Inner and Outer Skeletons

Which animal has more neck bones, a giraffe or a sparrow? Whose skeleton has hollow bones? Which bones are the largest and the tiniest in the human body? Which animals grow new skeletons? You will find the answers to these questions in this book.

An animal's skeleton is the rigid or semirigid part that supports soft tissues and protects important internal body organs.

Most living things have support. Some have support on the inside of their body, such as bones or *cartilage* that form an *endoskeleton*. Others have a hardened support on the outside, made of a horny or bony substance, called an *exoskeleton*.

Some animals have both an endoskeleton and an exoskeleton. Their exoskeleton is composed of *dermal* bones, or skin bones. Skin layers can store horny material in the form of claws, scales, feathers, hoofs, hair, teeth, and horns.

There are two divisions in the animal kingdom: animals with backbones, the *vertebrates*, and animals without backbones, the *invertebrates*. Actually, invertebrates don't have any bones at all.

The vertebrate's inner skeleton includes a backbone or spine. A spine is a row of bones under the skin along the middle

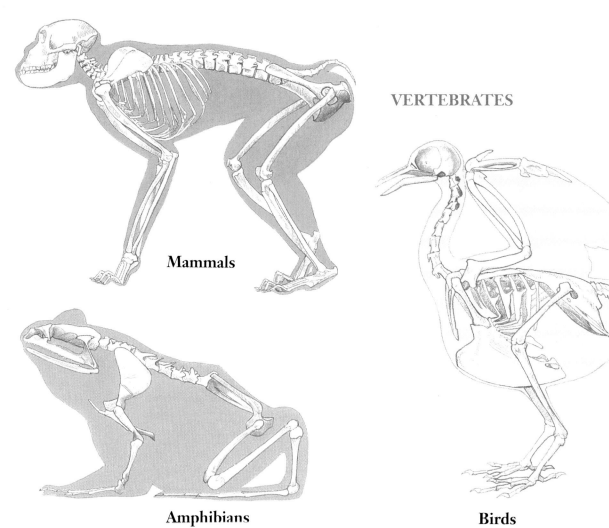

VERTEBRATES

Mammals

Amphibians

Birds

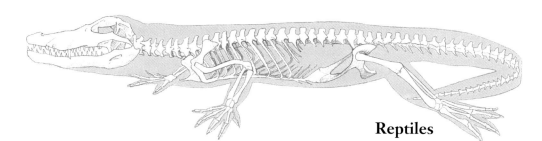

Reptiles

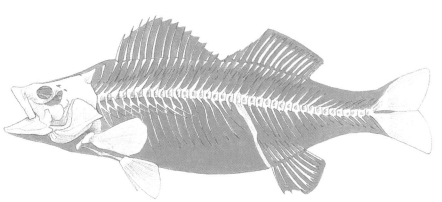

Fish

of the back. These bones are called *vertebrae*. The number of vertebrae can vary: a frog has nine, a human thirty-three, a snake four hundred. Other bones are attached to the spine and are also part of the skeleton.

The inner skeleton of vertebrates is organized into three groups of bones. One group runs down the middle of the body and includes the skull, backbone, and rib cage. A second group hangs or branches from the backbone and includes arms, legs, collarbone, and hips. The third group includes bones (such as tiny ear bones) that are inside cavities of the body.

All vertebrates follow a similar skeletal design of skull, backbone, ribs, and limbs. All, except snakes, have four limbs. Mammals, birds, reptiles, *amphibians*, and fish are vertebrates.

> Can you guess which vertebrate can hide inside its endoskeleton? (Answers to all questions can be found on page 60.)

The majority of animals are invertebrates, which do not have backbones or bony skeletons. Instead, they have hard body covers that protect their soft insides. Insects, spiders, *crustaceans*, *corals*, and *mollusks* have exoskeletons, or outer support.

Land invertebrates, such as insects, tend to be small, since their outer casings can sometimes be heavy. However, sea invertebrates, such as crabs and mollusks, can grow much larger; the water buoys up their skeletons and makes them feel lighter.

Vertebrates and invertebrates live on land and in the sea. Some even fly. No matter where creatures live, their skeletons serve specific functions: to shield the body, to act as a supporting framework, and to allow body movement.

INVERTEBRATES

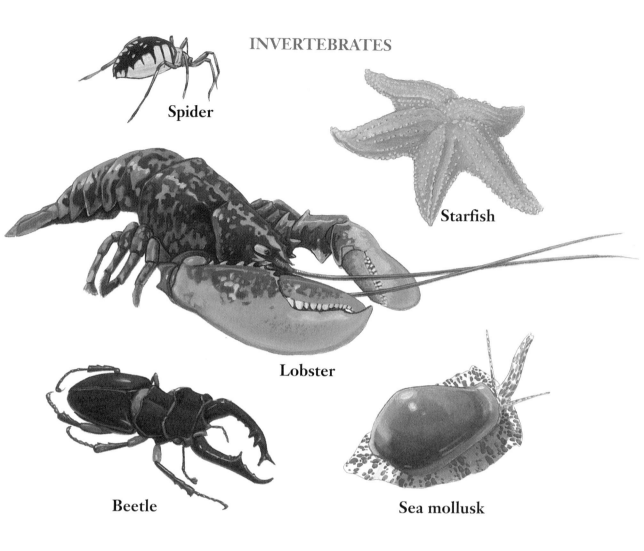

Spider

Starfish

Lobster

Beetle

Sea mollusk

ACTIVITIES

○ Rub your fingers along the middle of a human's or animal's back. The bumps you feel are the vertebrae.

○ Take a walk with a friend in your yard, neighborhood, or a park. Try to find and identify vertebrate animals and invertebrate animals.

two
Invertebrates: No Backbones

Most of the animals on earth are invertebrates, animals without backbones. These creatures range in size from microscopic plankton to immense corals, which are actually communities of small invertebrates.

Support of invertebrates' bodies comes in many different forms. The hard covering, or exoskeleton, can be plates, shells, thin casings, or stonelike substances. The exoskeleton supports the body from the outside in, rather than from the inside out. It also protects the invertebrate's internal organs from diseases, *predators*, and *parasites*.

AQUATIC INVERTEBRATES

Corals are tiny animals, called polyps, which have tubelike bodies with tentacles around their mouths. They produce a hard limestone to protect their soft bodies. As they multiply, the polyps grow their skeletons on the hard deposits of former corals that have gone before. These form reefs that can be more than a thousand miles long. The limestone skeletons of different kinds of coral are formed in a variety of shapes; some look like branches or antlers, some like shelves, and some like large boulders. Soft corals such as sea plumes and sea fans do not produce limestone coverings, but are supported by skeletons of embedded "needles" of limestone.

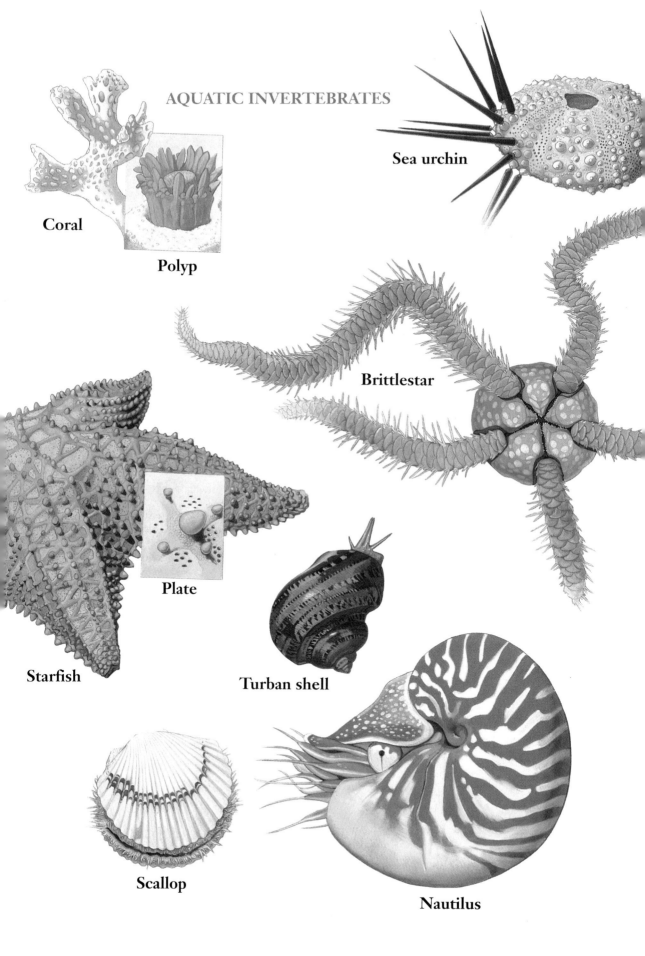

AQUATIC INVERTEBRATES

Coral

Polyp

Sea urchin

Brittlestar

Starfish

Plate

Turban shell

Scallop

Nautilus

Sea urchins, starfish, and brittlestars form a group called echinoderms, which means "spiny-skinned." They have plated exoskeletons made of *calcium carbonate.*

The sea urchin has a ball-shaped exoskeleton called a test. The test is made of many curved calcium plates. Each waving spine is attached to the spherical exoskeleton by a ball-and-socket joint.

The body of a starfish looks stiff, but it can bend and twist into different shapes to fit the outline of the ocean floor. Its body wall is embedded with a meshwork of thousands of tiny plates. The plates are like bones, with spaces and living cells. They are joined by a tough connective tissue that gives starfish a flexible skeletal frame. The brittlestar has many small spiny overlapping plates, which allow much flexibility.

Skeletal support and protection in mollusks also varies. Snails and conches have cone-shaped and whorled shells. Clams, cockles, and oysters are bivalves—they live inside two shells that hinge together. With growth, their exoskeletons show added rings, whorls, or ribs. Some mollusks that can propel themselves, such as squid and cuttlefish, have small internal shells for skeletons. Another propelling mollusk, the nautilus, has a coiled outer shell.

The exoskeletons of crustaceans such as shrimp, lobsters, and crabs have large amounts of calcium for added hardness. The joints of their exoskeletons have thin, flexible outer skin to allow easy movement.

LAND INVERTEBRATES

Crustaceans belong to a group of invertebrates called *arthropods.* Arthropod means "joint-legged." Eighty percent of animals alive on earth today are arthropods. Most arthropods, such as insects, spiders, and millipedes, live primarily on land. They have skeletons that encase their bodies in a horny layer. This exoskeleton is

LAND INVERTEBRATES

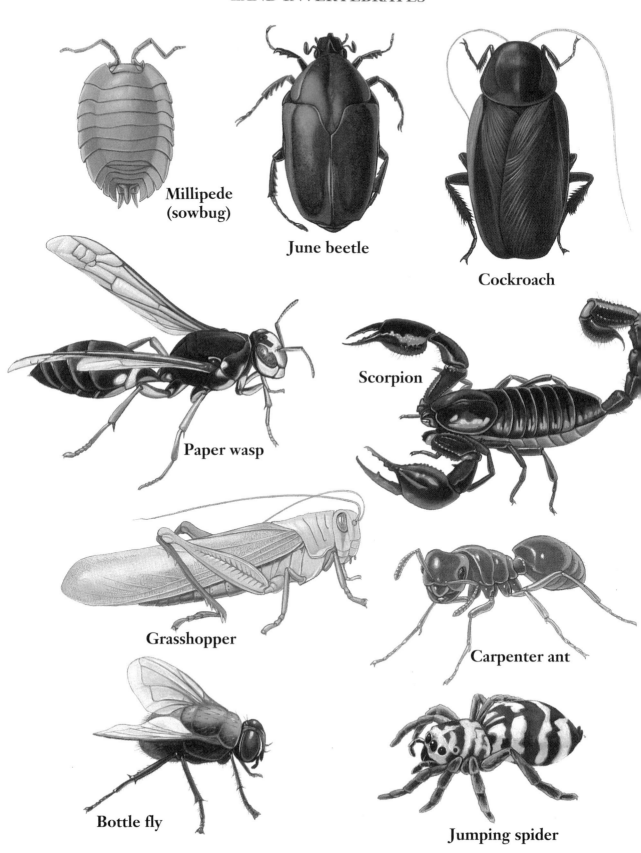

Millipede
(sowbug)

June beetle

Cockroach

Paper wasp

Scorpion

Grasshopper

Carpenter ant

Bottle fly

Jumping spider

made of a substance called *chitin*. This rigid, tough, but light-weight, material gives strength to the body. You might compare its flexibility and hardness to your fingernails.

In order to grow bigger, an arthropod must shed its exoskeleton and grow a new one. This molting is done by puffing its body out or hunching up and popping off its old covering. Although the new skeleton hardens quickly, the animal is temporarily without protection and must hide from predators.

The woodlouse, or pill bug, has a waxy-coated exoskeleton that is jointed so that it can roll itself into a ball for protection against predators like spiders.

True or false: The furry tarantula is really a mammal with an internal skeleton. (For answer see page 60.)

Insects have a thick waterproof layer on the outside of their segmented exoskeletons. Common insects include ants, cockroaches, flies, bees, termites, grasshoppers, and beetles. The skeletons of fleas and lice are tough, leathery skins that protect them when their hosts scratch.

The exoskeleton has three functions: It protects soft inner organs, supports the animal's body, and helps the animal to move.

ACTIVITIES
○ Collect insects that visit your yard, using a jar with holes in the lid. After observing their exoskeletons, let them go.
○ Get a baby snail. Keep it in a jar with wet flowers and leaves for food. See how fast it grows. Measure it each week.
○ If you can visit the beach, collect some empty seashells. Look for their growth lines and see their many shapes and sizes.

THIGHBONE AT HIP

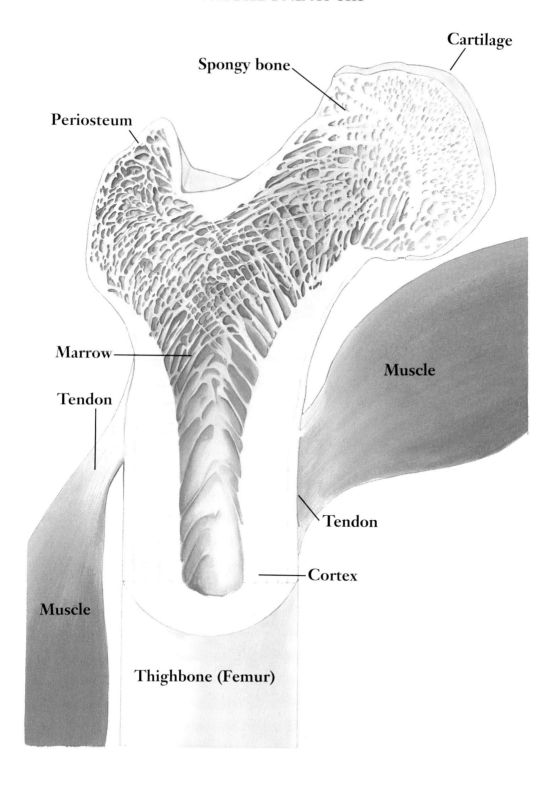

Cartilage

Spongy bone

Periosteum

Marrow

Tendon

Muscle

Tendon

Cortex

Muscle

Thighbone (Femur)

three
What's Inside Bone?

The skeletons of vertebrates are made mostly of bone. Bones are alive and growing inside their bodies. Human bones grow until a person is about twenty-five years old.

There are many shapes and sizes of bones. They can be smooth (skull), knobby (spine), curved (ribs), long (arms and legs), short (fingers and toes), heavy (pelvis or hips), and tiny (ear bones). Despite their differences in shape and size, all bones have a few common characteristics. They are hard, whitish, and more lasting than the rest of the body.

Bones have three layers. The outer layer, or *cortex*, is hard and strong. The surface of the cortex is surrounded by a membrane called the *periosteum*. Attached to the periosteum are stretchy *muscles* and binding *ligaments*. Both muscles and ligaments help in skeletal movement.

The middle layer of bone is spongy. This is where the blood deposits the calcium needed for healthy bone growth. The inner layer is a red fatty substance called *marrow*, where red and white blood cells are made. The marrow makes enough blood cells to completely replace a human's blood every three or four months.

Connecting bones would wear down at the ends if it weren't for the cartilage that is between them. Cartilage is a flexible whitish material that both links and cushions bones.

Unborn babies and small children have a lot of cartilage in the ends of their bones. It is eventually replaced by hard material. The cartilage in the nose and ears never becomes bone.

About one-fourth of bone is water. The rest is composed of blood vessels; nerves; marrow; calcium, phosphorus, and other minerals; and a stringy protein fiber called *collagen*. Phosphorus and calcium combine to make a mineral that makes bones "bony."

A bone is a project under endless construction. At the bone demolition site, *osteoclast* cells destroy old bone tissue by making tiny pinhead-size holes. The old bone is reabsorbed into the blood.

Builder cells, called *osteoblasts*, immediately fill the holes with collagen, which eventually hardens to new bone. This process is known as *calcification*. Osteoblasts are left behind in the bone to maintain it. They are then called *osteocytes*.

A MAGNIFIED CROSS SECTION OF BONE

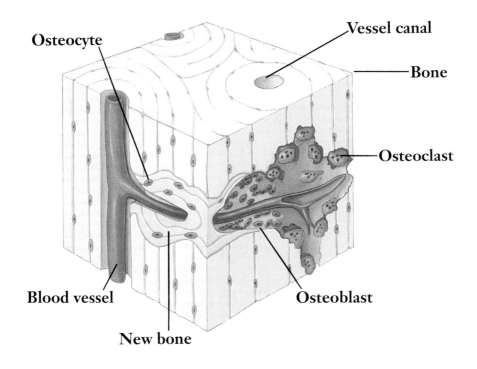

Osteocyte

Vessel canal

Bone

Osteoclast

Blood vessel

New bone

Osteoblast

Bone demolition and formation is happening at different stages throughout the skeleton. The constant renewal of bones is partly in reaction to the pressure of gravity. An astronaut's bones stop growing temporarily during space flight when there is practically no gravity.

With age or inactivity, bones can break more easily. When there is a break, blood vessels penetrate the bone to supply the necessary cells for repair.

True or false: Athletes have stronger bones because they exercise more. (For answer see page 60.)

Healthy bones depend on exercise and the food we eat. Activities such as running, jumping, skipping, climbing, and swimming help to keep our bones dense. A balanced diet of dairy products, leafy dark green vegetables, and bony fish will provide ample calcium.

ACTIVITY
How to Make a Bone Soft and Bendable
1. Remove the meat from a cooked or raw chicken or turkey drumstick bone. This bone is long and has knobs on the ends.
2. Soak the bone in a covered jar filled with distilled vinegar.
3. Every three days take the bone out and gently try to bend it. Put it back in the jar and, if necessary, refill with fresh vinegar. Note: A raw bone will turn the vinegar brown.
4. In about two weeks, the bone should be quite rubbery. You may even be able to tie it in a knot. What happened? Vinegar is a weak acid. It dissolved the calcium that made the bone rigid.

PERCH SKELETON

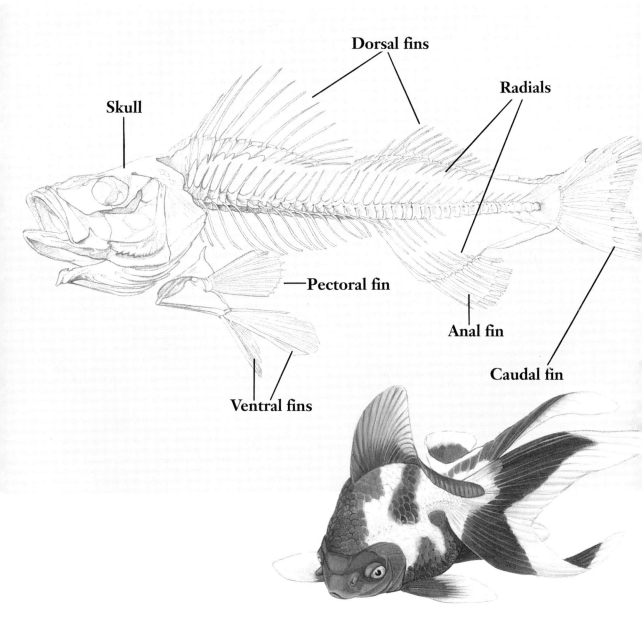

Dorsal fins

Radials

Skull

Pectoral fin

Anal fin

Caudal fin

Ventral fins

Goldfish have soft, flowing fins

four
Vertebrates: Backboned Animals

Bone and cartilage are found only in vertebrates. In many higher animals, the endoskeleton formed in the embryo is at first cartilaginous. As the animal matures, the cartilage changes into bone.

Some 400 million years ago, fish were the first vertebrates to appear on earth. Most fish have skeletons made of bone, but one group of fish has skeletons made of cartilage. Ninety percent of fish belong to the bony group. Some examples are goldfish, trout, perch, and halibut. Those in the cartilage group include sharks and rays.

When you eat fish, you'll notice that most of them have lots of fine bones. A bony fish endoskeleton is composed of the skull, backbone or spine, ribs, *radials*, and fins. The scales and bones of the skin in the head are part of the exoskeleton.

Thin winglike fins are used for swimming, balancing, and turning. Fins are located in different places along a fish's body. Fins such as the *dorsal*, *anal*, and *caudal* (tail) run along the middle of the body. They stick out vertically, or straight up and down, on the back, underside, and tail. The paired *pectoral* fins, which correspond to the *forelimbs* of a four-legged animal, are behind the skull. Behind those are the paired *ventral* pelvic fins.

Upper and lower fins are supported by bony spikes called radials, which are set firmly in the fish's body. The radials make the fins spread out or fold together. Some fins may be stiff with spikes. Others may be soft and flowing, like those on a fantail goldfish.

The backbone of the fish has one pair of ribs attached to each vertebra from the back of the head to the tail. Muscles along the backbone pull the fish's body, making it sway from side to side as it swims.

The skulls of early fish had no jaws. Fish sucked or sifted tiny bits of food from the mud. With the *evolution* of jaws and teeth, fish are able to grip and gulp their slippery prey.

The flounder family of fish, which includes the sole and halibut, undergoes an interesting skeletal change. When born, the pancake-shaped fish swims like a normal fish. While it is still less than one inch in length, it turns on its side, swimming in an up-and-down movement rather than side-to-side. Then an unusual change takes place. The eye on the lower side moves across the top of the head next to the eye on the upper side. The skull and mouth become twisted. The bottom side turns a whitish color while the top side matches its surroundings.

Why don't fish need as strong skeletons as land-living vertebrates? (For answer see page 60.)

A bony fish has a shield of scales made of the dermis layer of skin. These dermal scales contain bonelike material. On fish, scales will come off separately, like confetti, if you scrape them.

Sharks, skates, and rays have skeletons made of cartilage. A cartilaginous skeleton is softer than bone. It is tough but flexible, like the flexible cartilage of the human ear.

A shark's spinal column is composed of round *disks* of car-

THE FLOUNDER

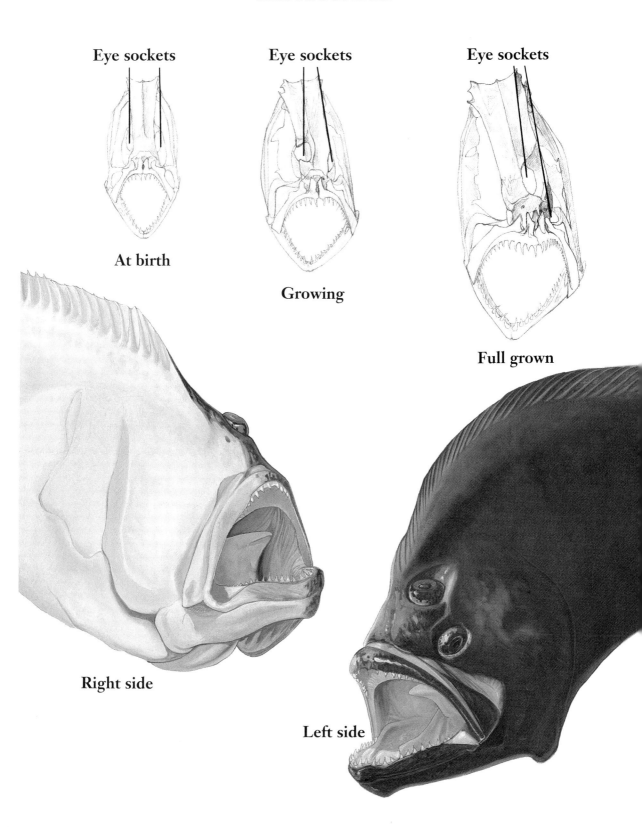

Eye sockets

At birth

Eye sockets

Growing

Eye sockets

Full grown

Right side

Left side

THE FLEXIBLE, CARTILAGINOUS
SHARK SKELETON

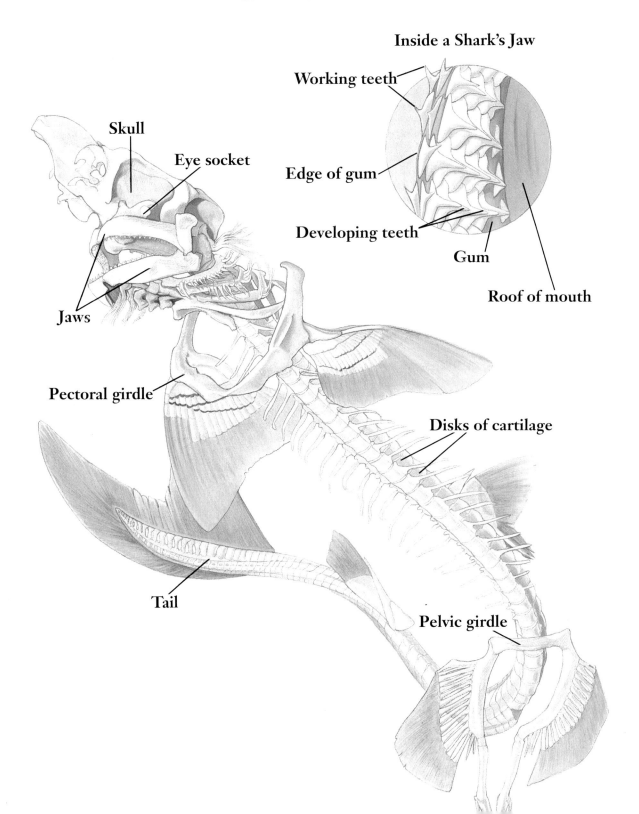

Skull

Eye socket

Inside a Shark's Jaw

Working teeth

Edge of gum

Developing teeth

Gum

Roof of mouth

Jaws

Pectoral girdle

Disks of cartilage

Tail

Pelvic girdle

tilage. Each disk contains calcium to make it hard. The shark's jaws and its many rows of teeth also contain calcium. These calcium-enriched body parts are the only remains that are preserved after a shark dies.

Cartilaginous fish are covered with denticles, or tiny teeth, which is a form of scale. Their skin feels like sandpaper and each tooth is almost as hard as your own teeth. Unlike most animals who stop growing when they reach adulthood, both bony and cartilaginous fish can grow throughout their life.

ACTIVITY

Have an adult help you with this activity. Go to a grocery store and buy a whole fish like sole, halibut, or perch. Try to identify its fins. Cook the fish and then cut it apart and look at its skeleton of bones. Before eating any meat, make sure all the bones are removed.

HOW A FROG GROWS

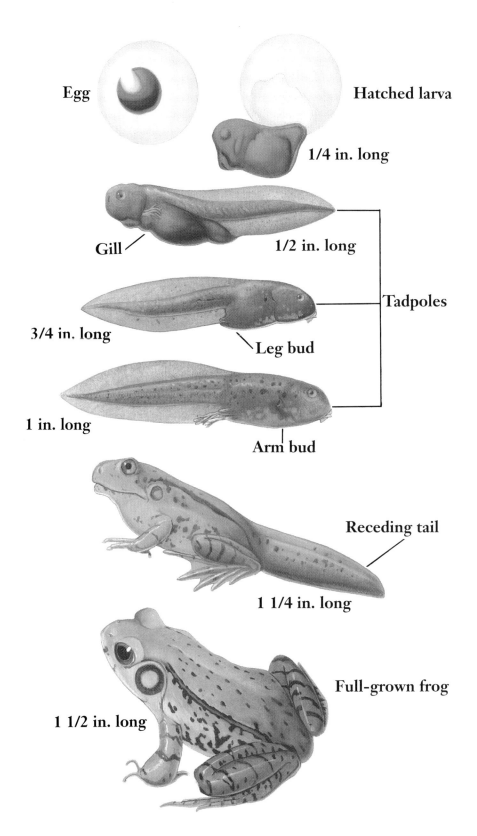

Egg

Hatched larva

1/4 in. long

Gill

1/2 in. long

Tadpoles

3/4 in. long

Leg bud

1 in. long

Arm bud

Receding tail

1 1/4 in. long

Full-grown frog

1 1/2 in. long

five
Amphibians: Double Life

Amphibians live both on land and in water. These and all four-limbed vertebrates evolved from fish. Some scientists believe that the fins of a certain prehistoric fish evolved into legs. The fish then could crawl onto land. This was the first amphibian.

Frogs, toads, and salamanders are amphibians. All amphibians are dependent on moisture. They cannot survive drying out.

The life cycle of amphibians is different from other vertebrates, whose young generally are born or hatched looking like miniature adults. Many amphibians start life as eggs in water. When they hatch, they are tadpoles or *larvae*, and they breathe with gills. Later they develop lungs and limbs and come on land.

FROGS AND TOADS

Frogs and toads are in the same family. A tadpole's skeleton is made of cartilage that changes to bone in the adult stage. Its legs develop while in the tadpole stage. The tadpole's tail shrinks since it is not needed on land.

The frog's skeleton has short front limbs, each with four toes. The three parts of the hind legs are the thigh, calf, and foot. They are about equal in length. As the frog leaps through the air,

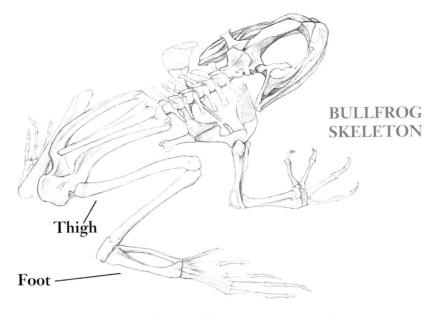

Thigh

Foot

each part of the leg unfolds. The short spine of eight or nine vertebrae keeps the frog stiff while leaping. Its long hind limbs have five toes with webbing in between. The toes spread open when the frog swims. This helps propel the frog through the water, the way rubber swim fins help you when you swim.

True or false: A frog's enormous eye sockets in the skull and bulging eyes help it eat. (For answer, see page 60.)

Nearly all frogs and toads catch prey with long sticky tongues that are attached at the front of their lower jaws. Their tongues unroll and shoot out to seize insects. They swallow their food whole.

THE FROG CATCHING PREY WITH ITS TONGUE

SALAMANDERS

Some people confuse salamanders with lizards, which are reptiles, not amphibians. The most noticeable difference between them is their skin. Lizards have a tough, horny layer of scales, while salamanders have smooth, scaleless skin. Salamanders have only one neck bone as do frogs and toads. A salamander has ribs down to the tail, as a fish does. Salamander skeletons do not change completely into bone. Wrist, ankle, chest, and pelvic bones remain as cartilage. Tail vertebrae are added throughout life.

Tail

MUD PUPPY SKELETON

Skull

ACTIVITY
Visit a pond to find amphibians. Can you find amphibians in their different life stages? Eggs? Tadpoles with a cartilaginous skeleton? Hopping frogs or toads with bony skeletons?

THE SALAMANDER FAMILY

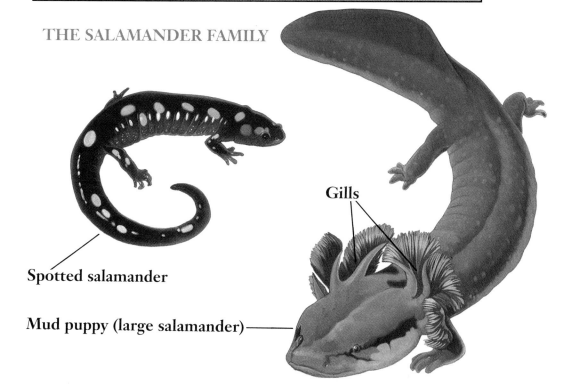

Gills

Spotted salamander

Mud puppy (large salamander)

THE ALLIGATOR

CROCODILE SKELETON

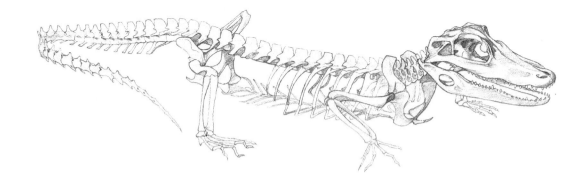

six
Reptiles: Creepers and Crawlers

Reptiles are vertebrates that move with short legs or on their bellies. Crocodiles and alligators, lizards, turtles, and snakes are reptiles. Their neck and back bones are parallel to the ground.

Reptiles' upper and lower jaws are U-shaped. The jaws fit nicely into each other. As they shift their jaws, back and forth, their food is gulped toward their throat. The teeth of crocodiles, snakes, and most lizards are continuously replaced. Although turtles lack teeth, they bite effectively with their horny beaks.

Which has more ribs, an 8-foot crocodile or a 2-foot snake? (For answer see page 60.)

CROCODILES AND ALLIGATORS

Crocodiles and alligators can be distinguished by their snouts; the alligator's is shorter and wider. The large flat skull of a crocodile is so heavy that it is a burden to carry on land. But in water the crocodile's body is buoyant, or able to float, and its head easier to support. Crocodiles and alligators, like birds, also have hollow cavities filled with air sacs, which help with floating. Their eye sockets and nostrils are placed high on top of the skull. This allows them to look for food, watch for enemies, and breathe while swimming.

Their powerful jaws are much like those of other vertebrates. The upper jaw is part of the skull, while the lower jaw is hinged to the skull for movement.

Crocodiles have nine bones in their necks. Their short limbs have three main parts like other vertebrates: the upper leg, lower leg, and foot. The spine is fused to the pelvis, which has thighbone sockets on the sides. This makes their legs stick out sideways, rather than under their bodies. Their toes are webbed for paddling in water and to keep them from sinking into soft mud. The long powerful tail swipes side to side for fast swimming. Crocodiles and alligators have thick horny skin composed of scales and plates.

LIZARDS

Most lizards have short necks, long slender bodies and tails, and four short legs. You may have seen some lizards such as the iguana, chameleon, and gecko in pet stores or a zoo.

Some interesting features of lizard skeletons include the chameleon's opposing, or facing, toes on each foot. Like the human's thumb, these opposing toes enable the foot to grasp tree branches as the lizard hunts insect prey.

Lizards that live in trees, such as the chameleon, have a long muscular *prehensile* tail, which means its tail can grasp branches. The prehensile tail is like a fifth limb.

Some lizards' tails break off, allowing them to escape from their enemies. There is a preset crack in the tail vertebrae and the nearby muscles are arranged to separate in a clean break. A new tail is grown by the lucky lizard.

Lizards curve their flexible spines from side to side when

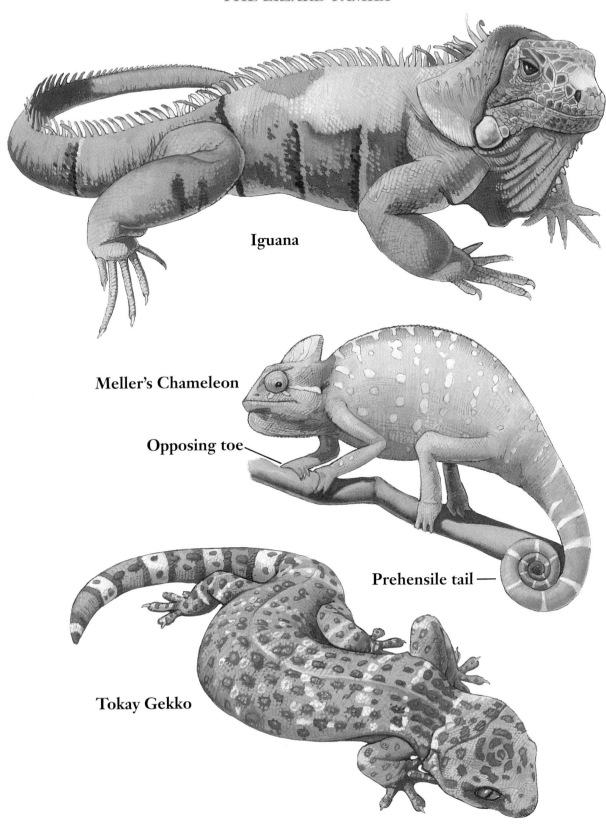

Iguana

Meller's Chameleon

Opposing toe

Prehensile tail

Tokay Gekko

LIZARD SKELETONS

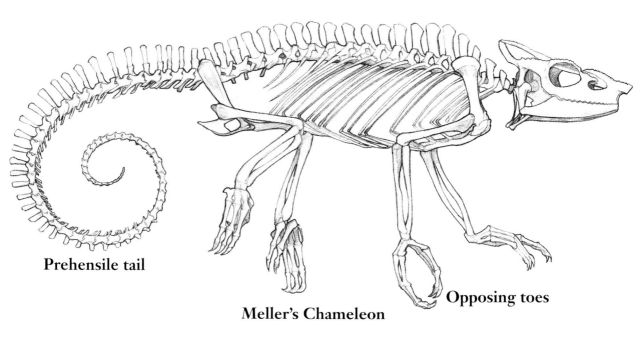

Prehensile tail

Meller's Chameleon

Opposing toes

Tegu Lizard, moving with a "swimming" walk

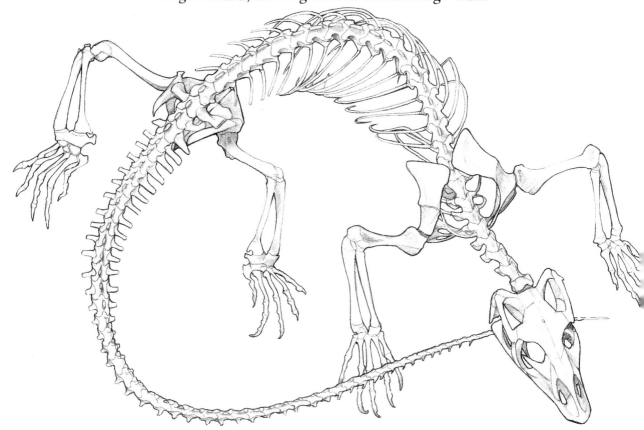

walking. They are said to have a "swimming" walk like a fish waving its spine to propel itself. The lizard has a tough, horny layer in its epidermis, which is sometimes arranged in colorful scales.

TURTLES AND TORTOISES

A turtle's skeleton is unique. The turtle has managed to grow most of its skeleton on the outside of its body, rather than inside. This inside-out skeleton allows it to retract its head, tail, and limbs inside the rib cage. The shell, a fused rib cage, is an endoskeleton. Over that is an exoskeleton—horny plates called scutes.

TURTLE SKELETON

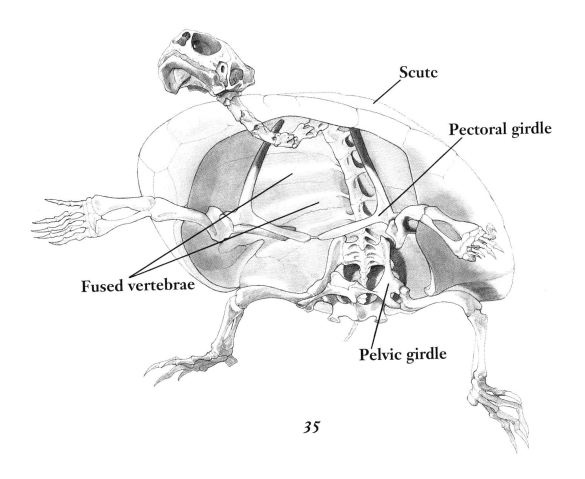

Scute

Pectoral girdle

Fused vertebrae

Pelvic girdle

The top shell, the *carapace*, and the bottom shell, the *plastron*, join together on the sides. The thick, hard shells account for 30 percent of the turtle's weight and make it awkward for the turtle to move quickly on land. The shell is not shed, but grows with the turtle. Sometimes you can see rings on the carapace scutes similar to tree rings. Each ring represents one year.

Turtles live both in water and on land. Sea turtles have flatter shells for skimming through water. Their legs have evolved into flippers. Most fresh water turtles have webbed toes for swimming. Claws on their toes are used for digging holes to lay their eggs in.

Land-dwelling turtles are usually called tortoises. Some tortoises have rounded upper shells. Their thick hind legs look like elephants' legs. Their limbs are covered with hard scales and are adapted for walking rather than swimming.

GIANT TORTOISE

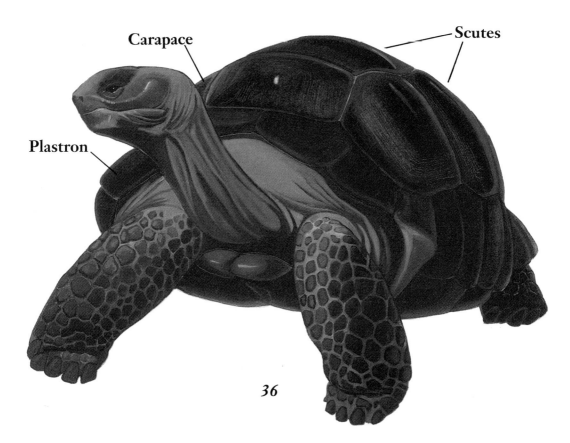

Carapace

Scutes

Plastron

36

RED-EARED SLIDER

MARINE TURTLE

Scutes

SNAKES

A snake's skeleton is all backbone and ribs connected to a skull. Snakes have between 160 and 400 vertebrae and almost as many pairs of ribs.

The skeleton is lightweight for freedom of movement. Snakes have no limbs, but can climb, swim, and burrow. They move by using their rib muscles and belly scales. The scales slant downward to grip the surface.

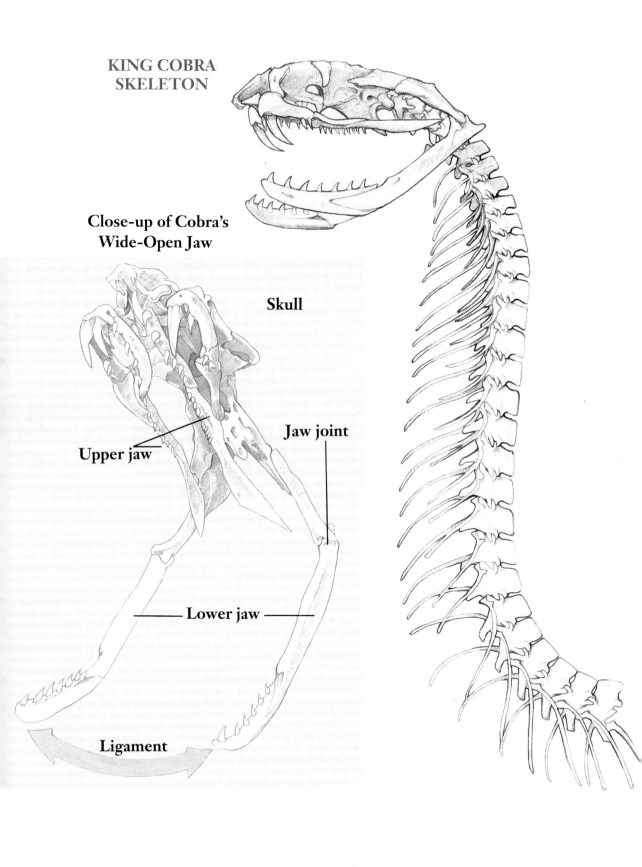

KING COBRA
SKELETON

Close-up of Cobra's
Wide-Open Jaw

Skull

Upper jaw

Jaw joint

Lower jaw

Ligament

The skull is loosely built and can be stretched in several directions. The upper jaw has four rows of teeth and the lower jaw two rows of teeth. All the teeth point backward to hook prey into the mouth and throat, as the food moves slowly to the stomach. Many snakes are able to separate their jaw joints. This allows them to open their mouths enormously wide. Some large snakes, like the python, can even eat a small antelope.

The snake crawls out of its entire epidermis each growth period. You may have seen a shedded snake skin, which is almost transparent and petal-thin. Reptile scales come from the epidermis layer, which peels off in pieces as your own epidermis does after a bad sunburn.

When you hear the rattle of a snake's tail, you are not hearing his tail bones. The rattlesnake's tail is really rings of hardened skin, left after molting.

ACTIVITY

Try to visit a live reptile exhibit where you can see a variety of lizards, turtles, and snakes. Look for a chameleon's opposing toes and prehensile tail, and a tortoise's domed shell. Perhaps you'll be lucky enough to see a snake's stretched and humped body showing a recent meal, or maybe even a snake skin that has been shed.

CHICKEN SKELETON

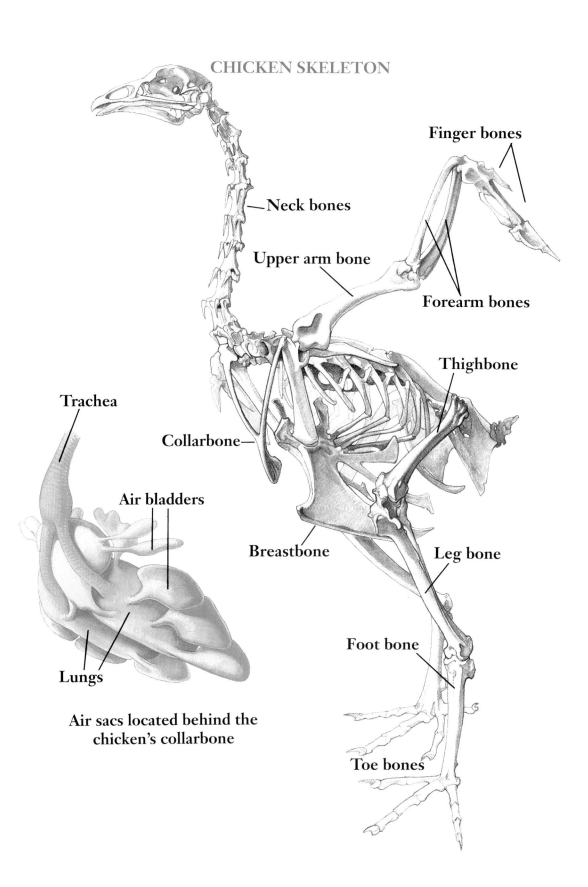

Finger bones

Neck bones

Upper arm bone

Forearm bones

Thighbone

Trachea

Air bladders

Collarbone

Breastbone

Leg bone

Lungs

Foot bone

Air sacs located behind the
chicken's collarbone

Toe bones

seven
Birds: Hollow Bones

Birds are the only vertebrates with feathered bodies. Their forelimbs have been altered into wings. Bird skeletons differ from other vertebrates in one particular way. Many of the bones are hollow, like a drinking straw.

Hollow bones make a bird's body lighter for flying. The empty bones have thin crosswise inner supports to keep them hard. The skull, with its many gaps, is also airy and light. Birds have air sacs throughout their bodies. Air sacs add oxygen and enable birds to float on water. Hollow bones, gaps, and air sacs all play an important role in helping birds carry their weight when flying.

A bird's body must be rigid in order to fly. The vertebrae between the base of the neck and tail are fused together in one piece. It is similar to the body of an airplane.

The structure of a bird's wing is similar to a mammal's forelimb, but it lacks fourth and fifth digits, or fingers. Flight feathers are attached to the bird's forearm, wrist, and hand bones. Speed-control feathers are attached to the bird's first finger. Steering is done with tail feathers. The feather is composed of epidermis, the same horny material as reptile scales. Birds, like reptiles, have scales on their legs.

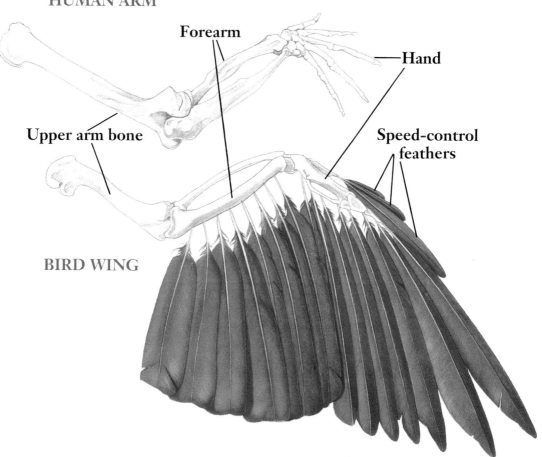

HUMAN ARM

Forearm

Hand

Upper arm bone

Speed-control
feathers

BIRD WING

Bird wing shapes have been copied by airplane designers.
The wings of crop-dusting and stunt planes, which make short
flights, are copied from the stubby-winged quail and pheasant.
Jet fighter planes are like swallows, whose wings are broad at the
body and pointed at the ends for fast quick turns. Gliders look
like the albatross and gull that ride the ocean winds with long
narrow wings. Jetliners have wings that separate on the edges for
balance and control like the wings of condors and vultures.

You can guess how a bird gets its food by the shape of its
beak. Birds with sharp pointed beaks, such as woodpeckers,
thrushes, and robins, peck at insects, grubs, and berries.

Birds with short, thick, cone-shaped beaks, such as parrots, crack and split seeds. Hooked-beaked birds, such as vultures, tear flesh from small animals. Birds with long, pointed bills, such as herons, scoop and spear fish.

Most swans and ducks have flat broad bills with fine horny ridges on the edges to strain underwater plants and small aquatic animals. Besides eating, birds also use their beaks for drinking, carrying nesting material, fighting, grooming, and breathing.

Of all the animals in the vertebrate category, birds have the most neck bones. They range from thirteen in pigeons to twenty-four in swans. The extra bones allow a bird to turn its head in all directions for watching enemies, feeding, preening, cleaning, and arranging its feathers.

Wood thrush

Pileated woodpecker

Blue macaw (parrot)

Bateleur (vulture)

Black-crowned night heron

Lesser scaup (duck)

Attached to the base of the neck, the two slender collarbones join together to form a V in front of the breast.

> What is another name for a bird's collarbone?
> (Hint: Think about Thanksgiving. Answer is on page 60.)

At the front of the body, a bird's ribs attach to a huge breastbone forming a shield across the chest. The breastbone anchors the strong wing-flapping muscles.

Some birds perch, some swim, some climb, and some walk. You can tell which they do by looking at their clawed feet.

A perching bird, such as a robin or thrush, has three toes in the front and one long toe in the back. Swimming birds, such as ducks and swans, have three webbed toes. Birds who climb, such as woodpeckers, have two front toes and two back toes. A walking bird, such as a chicken, has three front toes and one short back toe. Eagles and hawks have sharp talons for grasping prey.

> ## ACTIVITY
> Sit in your yard, in a park, at the beach, or go to a zoo aviary to observe birds. Look at their beaks and try to guess what they eat. Look at their feet. Are they perching, swimming, climbing, or walking birds? Can you identify their wings? Are they short-flight birds, rapid-turning birds, gliding birds, or jetliner birds?

COMPARING BIRD FEET

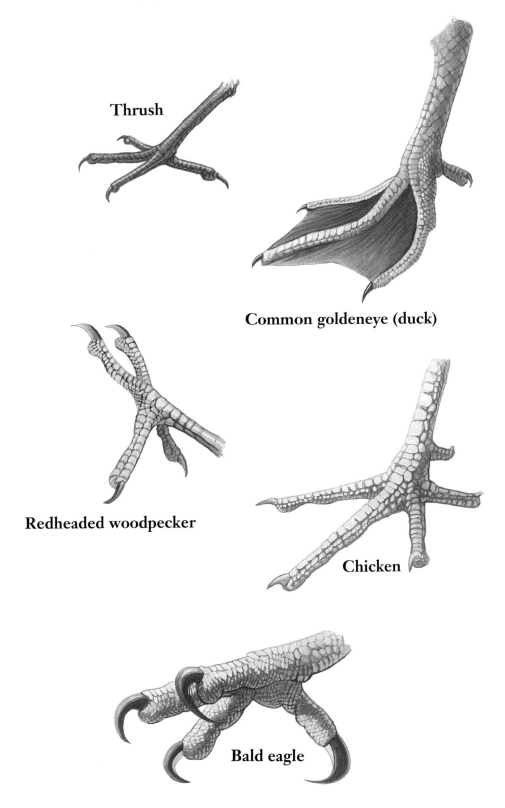

Thrush

Common goldeneye (duck)

Redheaded woodpecker

Chicken

Bald eagle

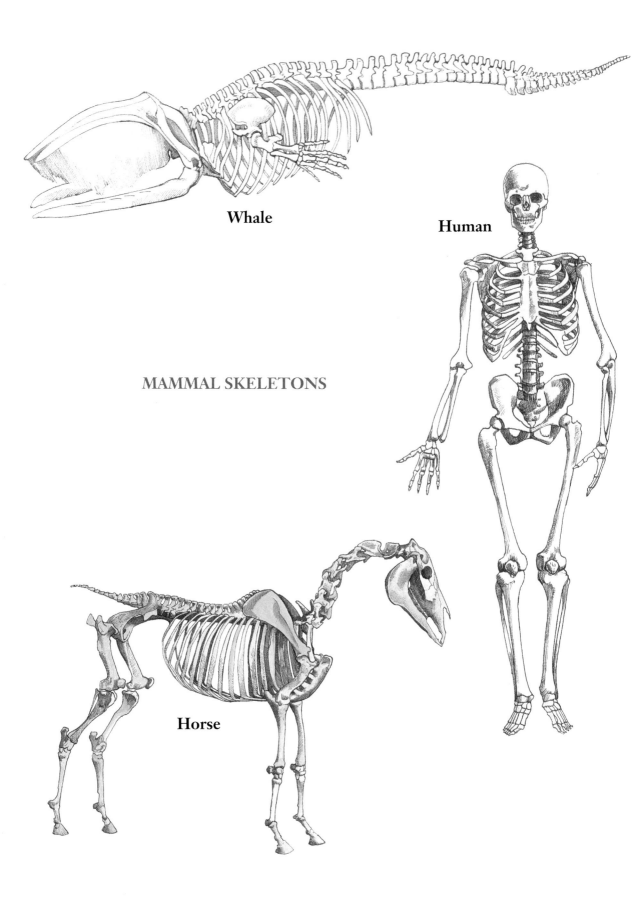

Whale

Human

MAMMAL SKELETONS

Horse

eight
Mammals: Our Own Family

The highest class of vertebrates is mammals, whose newborn offspring are fed milk from their mother. Humans, cats, dogs, horses, bats, elephants, giraffes, whales, dolphins, and sea lions are examples of mammals.

Mammals can weigh less than a dime—the shrew, for example. Other mammals, such as the whale, can weigh more than one hundred tons.

All mammals have the same skeletal pattern but their bones are different in size and function. Bones in mammals differ in number, shape, and weight.

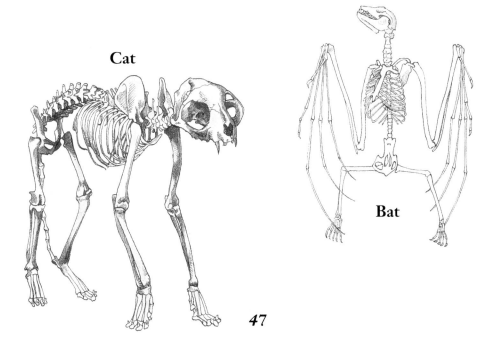

Cat

Bat

Compare the forelimb in the human, whale, bat, horse, and cat. The same basic bones are present in each animal. A human has long arms with hands and fingers that can pick up things. A whale's swimming paddle is short and thick.

The bat's wing bones are slender, long, and as delicate as toothpicks. In the horse's leg, its third finger and toe form a hoof. Even though cats walk on their toes, they have the same leg structure as humans.

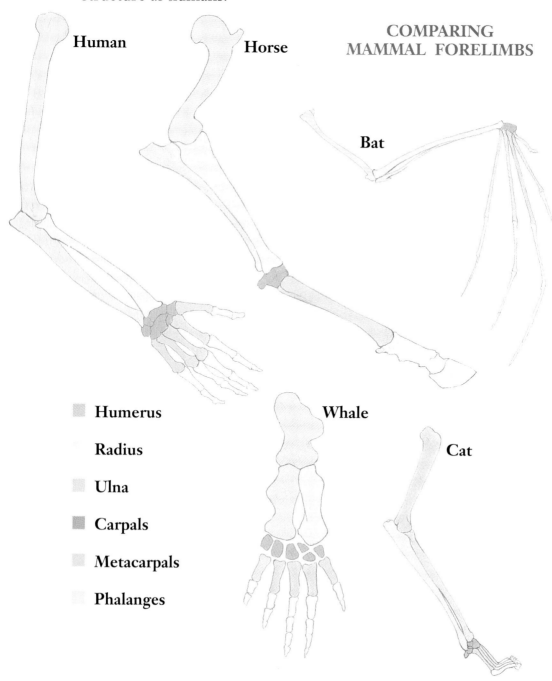

COMPARING MAMMAL FORELIMBS

Human

Horse

Bat

Humerus

Radius

Ulna

Carpals

Metacarpals

Phalanges

Whale

Cat

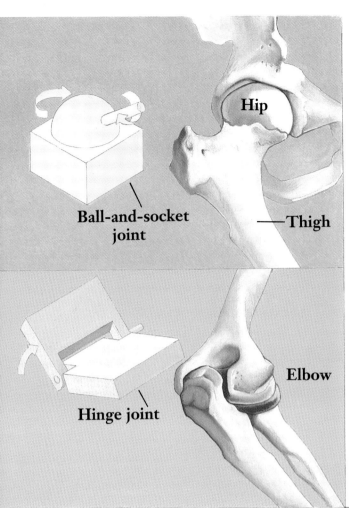

Ball-and-socket joint

Hip

Thigh

Hinge joint

Elbow

HOW DIFFERENT TYPES OF JOINTS WORK

Each bone in your body is joined to other bones by means of connective tissue. Bones meet at *joints*, which allow the body to move, bend, and twist. *Ball-and-socket* joints, such as the shoulders and hips, allow movement in any direction. *Hinge* joints, such as the knee, elbow, fingers, and toes, bend in only one direction, like a door does.

Gliding joints, such as wrists, ankles, and parts of the backbone, slide against each other. In a *pivot* joint, one bone pivots inside the other. The pivot joint in the neck allows the head to turn and nod.

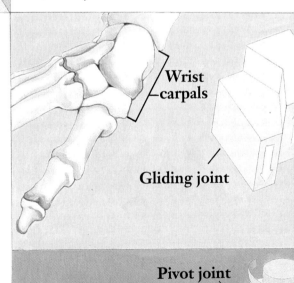

Wrist carpals

Gliding joint

Pivot joint

Vertebrae attached to head and neck

Look more closely at the human skeleton on the facing page. It has 206 bones. The skeleton weighs around one-tenth of the total body weight. If you weigh seventy pounds, your skeleton weighs about seven pounds.

The human skull has twenty-nine bones. The smooth brain case is made up of eight separate bones. Gaps in a baby's brain case allow room for the brain to grow.

The skull has eye sockets, ear holes, a nose hole, and a movable lower jawbone. These protect the organs of sight, hearing, smell, and taste. The skull is a combination of both endoskeletal and exoskeletal bones. The exoskeletal bones of the skull are the cheekbones and jawbones, the upper palate, and teeth. They are exoskeletal even though they are formed under the skin.

Teeth are not actually bones. But they are made of a bone-like material called *dentine*. Bone contains cell spaces but dentine does not, because the cells that made it moved away and weren't trapped inside the bone. Since teeth are anchored into the jawbone by roots, they are often shown in skeletons. Jaws and teeth give many clues about an animal. They tell what kind of food it eats and its age.

Herbivorous animals, like horses, cows, elephants, camels, giraffes, and deer, eat plant materials. They have broad flat molars for chewing and jaws that move sideways, up and down, and slide front to back for grinding.

Carnivorous animals, such as lions, tigers, cats, and dogs, eat meat. Their teeth are pointed for gripping, stabbing, cutting, and cracking bone. Their thick, heavy jaws move only up and down.

Humans are *omnivorous*, and can eat all kinds of food. They have both flat molars for grinding and sharp *incisors* for gripping. The lower jaw in humans moves up and down, side to side, and front to back.

THE BONES IN THE HUMAN SKELETON

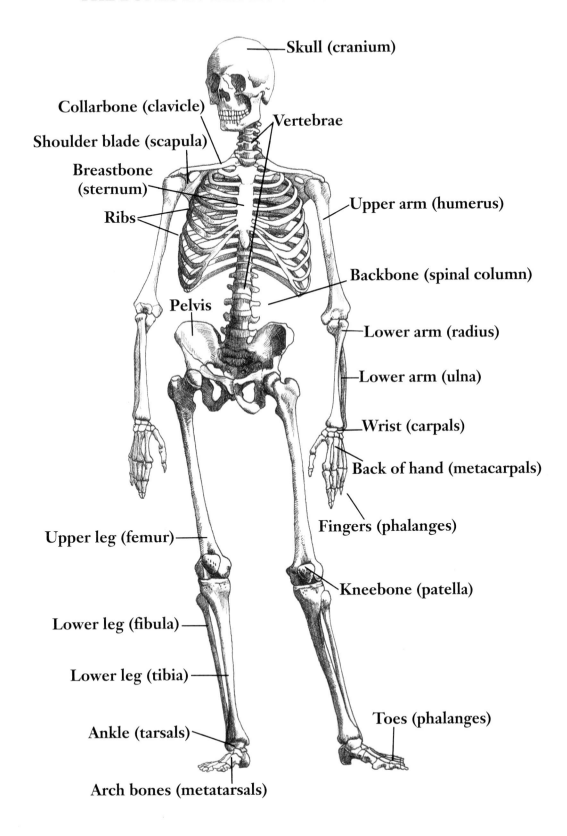

Skull (cranium)

Collarbone (clavicle)

Shoulder blade (scapula)

Breastbone (sternum)

Ribs

Vertebrae

Upper arm (humerus)

Backbone (spinal column)

Pelvis

Lower arm (radius)

Lower arm (ulna)

Wrist (carpals)

Back of hand (metacarpals)

Fingers (phalanges)

Upper leg (femur)

Kneebone (patella)

Lower leg (fibula)

Lower leg (tibia)

Toes (phalanges)

Ankle (tarsals)

Arch bones (metatarsals)

Some mammals have teeth that never stop growing. Can you guess which ones? (For answer see page 60.)

The backbone, or spine, of vertebrates is formed by linked bones that stretch from the skull to the tail. Each bone or vertebra is similar to a spool with knobs. The spinal cord runs through a hole in each lined-up vertebra. The number of vertebrae is not the same for all mammals.

The angle at which neck bones come out of the skull determines the posture of a vertebrate. In reptiles, such as lizards and snakes, and in fish, the neck and spine exits straight behind the skull. This forces the animal's head to be level with its body. It moves by crawling or swimming.

The neck and spine of four-legged mammals exits the skull at a downward angle from horizontal. This allows them to hold their heads higher than their body.

In humans, the neck and spine exit directly below the skull. Humans hold their heads on top of their body and walk upright.

The top seven bones of the human spine make up the neck. Interestingly, a giraffe has the exact same number of neck bones as a human and most other mammals, while a five-inch sparrow has fourteen bones in its neck.

The human spine is S-shaped with thirty-three vertebrae, the last four being fused into a tail bone. A cat has many separate tail bones that move freely. Its long tail helps it keep its balance when jumping or walking on a fence.

Attached to the human backbone are twelve pairs of ribs, which encircle the lungs and heart.

The bottom of the backbone is attached to the bowl-shaped hip or pelvic bone. The *pelvis* protects lower body organs such as the intestines, bladder, and in women, the uterus and other reproductive organs.

HUMAN SKULL AND SPINE

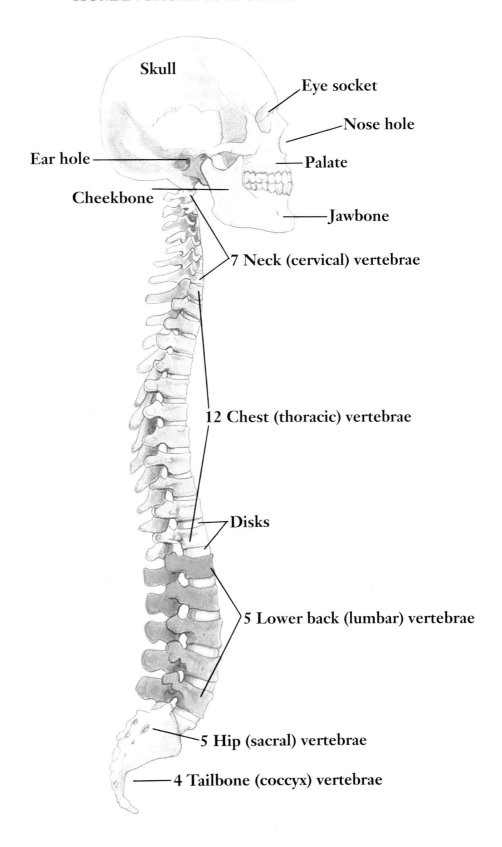

Skull

Eye socket

Nose hole

Ear hole

Palate

Cheekbone

Jawbone

7 Neck (cervical) vertebrae

12 Chest (thoracic) vertebrae

Disks

5 Lower back (lumbar) vertebrae

5 Hip (sacral) vertebrae

4 Tailbone (coccyx) vertebrae

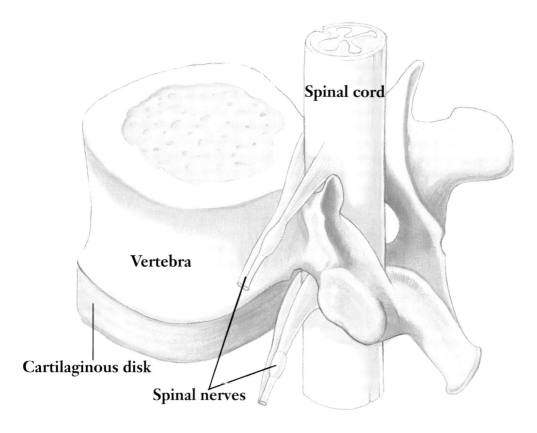

Spinal cord

Vertebra

Cartilaginous disk

Spinal nerves

CLOSE-UP OF ONE VERTEBRA

The pelvis has two cup-shaped sockets for the thighbones. This upper leg bone is the largest bone in the human body. In a six-foot-tall person, the thighbone, or femur, can be 20 inches (.5 meter) long. In contrast, the tiniest bones in the human body are the three ear bones: the anvil, hammer, and stirrup. The stirrup bone is .12 inch (3 millimeters)—about the width of one grain of rice.

Every part of the coverings of a vertebrate is derived from either the epidermal (outer) or dermal (inner) layers of the skin.

Hoofs of the horse, deer, and rhinoceros are all hardened

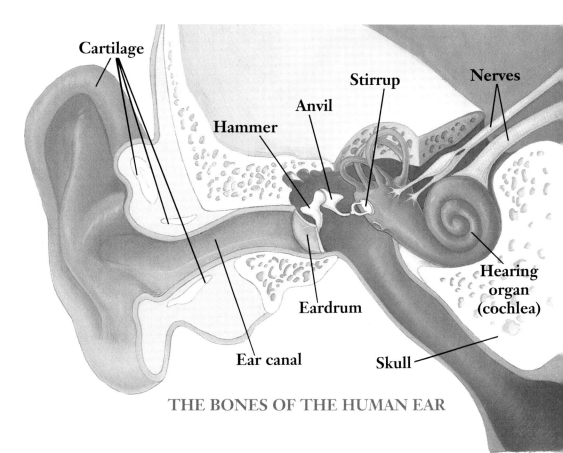

Cartilage

Stirrup

Nerves

Anvil

Hammer

Hearing organ (cochlea)

Eardrum

Ear canal

Skull

THE BONES OF THE HUMAN EAR

outer skin layers. So are the claws of cats and dogs, and human fingernails and toenails.

Sheep, cattle, and goat horns are never shed. They consist of hard epidermis fitting over a core of bone that grows out of the skull. Giraffe "horns" are made of true bone, covered with skin and hair.

Antlers on male deer and female reindeer are branched bone, which is shed each year. Each spring a new set of antlers grows from the old stumps. Mammal fur and hair are made of the epidermal layer of the skin and are similar to the horny material of scales. Some mammals, like beavers and rats, have scales in their tails.

All animals evolved in an orderly way and are related to each other. As different animals evolved, parts were added, subtracted, and multiplied. Some animals added vertebral bones. Hind legs in the whale's ancestors faded away. Muscles of ancient fish split up to control new limbs. Some bones fused together. Some parts shifted to new jobs. Gill bars, for example, became jaws, ear ossicles, and voice box.

Every inch of an animal is an adaptation. Whether vertebrate or invertebrate, each animal's skeleton is adapted, or fitted, to its own special use and for its own survival.

ACTIVITY
Feel your own bones, matching the shapes with the illustration of the human skeleton.

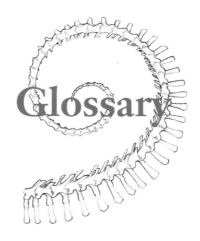

Glossary

amphibian (am-FI-bee-uhn)—an animal that can live both on land and in the water

anal (AY-nul)—referring to the hindmost fin of a fish

arthropod (AR-thruh-pod)—any animal without a backbone having a segmented body, jointed limbs, and a shell that is shed periodically

calcification (kal-suh-fuh-KAY-shun)—the hardening of a bone caused by the deposition of calcium salts

calcium carbonate (KAL-see-um KAR-buh-nate)—chemical compound that constitutes chalk

carapace (KAR-uh-pase)—a bony or horny case or shield covering all or part of the back of an animal (as a turtle)

carnivorous (kar-NI-vuh-rus)—meat-eating; feeding on flesh

cartilage (KAR-tul-ij)—a tough, flexible substance that forms part of the bodies of humans and animals; gristle

caudal (KAW-dal)—referring to the tail fin of a fish

chitin (KIE-tun)—a horny substance that forms part of the hard outer body covering of insects and crustaceans

collagen (KAH-luh-jun)—a fibrous protein of connective tissue and of bone

coral (KORE-ul)—a tiny sea animal that forms an outer skeleton of limestone *cortex* (KORE-teks)—the outer layer of bone

crustacean (krus-TAY-shun)—a creature that has no backbone, but a hard outer shell, and lives in the water

dentine (DEN-teen)—the main material of which teeth are made

dermal (DUR-mul)—relating to the layer of skin just below the outer skin

disk—a round, thin object

dorsal (DORE-sul)—near or on the back

endoskeleton (en-doh-SKEH-luh-tun)—the inner bones as the framework of the body

evolution (eh-vuh-LOO-shun)—a gradual, continuing development

exoskeleton (ek-soh-SKEH-luh-tun)—the hard outside covering of some animals, such as the shells of lobsters and shrimp or the covering of grasshoppers

forelimb (FOR-lim)—front extensions of the body used for moving or holding, as the arms

herbivorous (er-BIH-vuh-rus *or* her-BIH-vuh-rus)—feeding on plants rather than on animals

incisor (in-SIGH-zur)—a front tooth that has a sharp edge used for cutting

invertebrate (in-VER-tuh-brate)—an animal without a backbone

joint—the joining of two bones, especially where movement occurs, as the elbow joint, the knee joint

larva (LAR-vuh)—the early form of any animal that goes through several stages before it becomes an adult

ligament (LIH-guh-munt)—a band of tough tissue that holds bones together or gives support to other parts of the body

marrow (MAR-oh)—a soft substance in the centers of most bones; it contains fat and developing blood cells

mollusk (MAH-lusk)—animals, such as clams and snails, that have soft bodies, usually protected by a shell

muscle (MUH-sul)—body tissue which can be tightened or relaxed to cause movement *omnivorous* (om-NIH-vuh-rus)—eating both plant and meat foods

osteoblast (OS-tee-uh-blast)—a bone-forming cell

osteoclast (OS-tee-uh-klast)—a large multinuclear cell which absorbs bony tissue, forming hollow parts in the bone

osteocyte (OS-tee-uh-site)—a cell that maintains bone after it has formed.

parasite (PAR-uh-site)—a plant or animal that lives off another plant or animal without contributing anything in return

pectoral (PEK-tuh-rul)—situated in, near, or on the chest

pelvis (PEL-vus)—a basin-shaped area enclosed by the hipbones at the lower end of the backbone

periosteum (per-ee-OS-tee-um)—a membrane that surrounds bone

plastron (PLAS-trun)—the bottom shell of a turtle

predator (PREH-duh-tur)—an animal that catches and eats other animals

prehensile (pre-HEN-sul)—capable of grasping, especially by wrapping around

radials (RAY-dee-ulz)—bones in fish lying along a bodily radius; they support the fins

ventral (VEN-trul)—of or having to do with the belly

vertebra (VER-tuh-bruh) (plural *vertebrae* VER-tuh-bray)—one of the bony or cartilaginous segments composing the spinal column

vertebrate (VER-tuh-brate)—any animal with a spinal column

Answers to Questions

Page 9:   A turtle

Page 15:   False. The tarantula is an invertebrate with an exo-skeleton covered with soft fur.

Page 19:   True. Exercising our muscles pulls and puts stress on our bones. The bones respond by growing stronger and heavier.

Page 22:   Because fish are supported by the water in which they live.

Page 28:   True. Their eyeballs push food down their throats by bulging into the roof of their mouth. If you watch them eat, you will notice they blink as they swallow.

Page 31:   Crocodiles have nine pairs of ribs. Snakes have 100 to 400 pairs of ribs.

Page 44:   A wishbone

Page 52:   The teeth of squirrels, hamsters, mice, rabbits, guinea pigs, walruses, elephants, and beavers continue to grow throughout life. These animals need to gnaw on hard food, like nuts and seeds, carrots or wood, to keep their teeth worn down.

For Further Reading

Bender, Lionel. *Invertebrates.* New York: Gloucester Press, 1988.

Johnson, Sylvia A. *Coral Reefs.* Minneapolis: Lerner Publications, 1984.

Landau, Elaine. *Interesting Invertebrates: A Look at Some Animals without Backbones.* New York: Franklin Watts, 1991.

Parker, Steve. *Skeleton.* New York: Alfred A. Knopf, 1988.

Parker, Steve. *The Skeleton and Movement.* New York: Franklin Watts, 1989.

Ward, Brian. *Bones and Joints and Their Care.* New York: Franklin Watts, 1991.

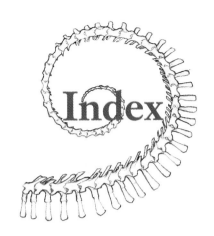

Index

About the Author

Judith Janda Presnall spent her childhood in Milwaukee, Wisconsin. She has a bachelor's degree in education from the University of Wisconsin in Whitewater. After twenty years of teaching, Judy now devotes her time to writing for children.

She and her husband, Lance, live in Los Angeles, California. They have a daughter, Kaye, and a son, Kory.

Judy has received awards from both the Society of Children's Book Writers & Illustrators and the California Writers Club for her children's nonfiction. Her previous book for Watts, *Animals That Glow*, won a 1994 National Science Teachers Association award for outstanding science trade book for children.